P9-DBK-372

Cornerstones of Freedom

The Trail of Tears

R. Conrad Stein

CP CHILDRENS PRESS®

CHICAGO

FRANKLIN PIERCE
COLLEGE LIBRARY
RINDGE, N.H. 03461

CURR
LE
99
.C5
S865
1993

Library of Congress Cataloging-in-Publication Data

Stein, R. Conrad.
  The trail of tears / by Conrad Stein.
    p. cm. — (Cornerstones of freedom)
  Summary: Describes the Federal government's seizure
of Cherokee lands in Georgia and the forced migration
of the Cherokee Nation to Oklahoma along the route
that came to be known as the Trail of Tears.
  ISBN 0-516-06666-8
  1. Cherokee Removal, 1838—Juvenile
literature. 2. Cherokee Indians—History—Juvenile
literature. [1. Cherokee Removal, 1838. 2. Cherokee
Indians—History. 3. Indians of North America—
Southern States—History.] I. Title. II. Series.
E99.C5S865 1993
975.004975—dc20   92-33422
[B]   CIP
                                                AC

Copyright 1993, 1985 by Childrens Press®, Inc.
Revised Edition, 1993.
All rights reserved. Published simultaneously in Canada.
Printed in the United States of America.
     2 3 4 5 6 7 8 9 10 R 02 01 00 99 98 97 96 95 94

Campfires flickered and elderly chiefs of various tribes sat cross-legged waiting to hear a speech from the famous Shawnee leader Tecumseh. He had called the council to discuss the survival of the Indian people.

"Where today are the Pequot?" Tecumseh asked. "Where are the Narragansett, the Mohican, the Pokanoket, and many other once powerful tribes of our people? They have vanished before the oppression of the white man. . . . Will we let ourselves be destroyed in our turn . . . without a struggle, give up our homes, our country, the graves of our dead, and everything that is dear and sacred to us? I know you will cry with me, 'Never! Never!' "

The chiefs nodded in agreement. For nearly two hundred years, the Indian population had dwindled as whites pushed steadily westward. White pioneers had a burning thirst for new land, a thirst that seemed unquenchable. Tecumseh believed that only if the various Indian tribes joined together would they be able to resist white expansion. He dreamed of an Indian alliance that would stretch like an iron belt from

The great Shawnee leader Tecumseh

When Tecumseh was killed in battle in 1813 (above), the dream of a united Indian nation died with him.

the Great Lakes to the Floridas and lock the whites into their eastern settlements.

But Tecumseh was killed in battle in 1813. With him died the dream of an Indian united front. No other leader of the time had the diplomatic skills necessary to mold the rival tribes into a confederation powerful enough to withstand the invasion of white settlers. Tecumseh's death meant that the settlers would face only scattered tribal resistance to their continuing drive into traditional Indian land. Some of the most desirable Indian land lay in the southeastern United States. Many of the Indians of that region—including the Cherokee, Creek, Choctaw, Chickasaw, and Seminole—had adopted some of the white settlers' ways. Whites called these groups the "Five Civilized Tribes" because they considered the societies of these groups to be more "advanced" than those of Indian groups that did not practice European customs.

Portraits of prominent members of four of the so-called "Five Civilized Tribes" (clockwise from top left): Seminole chief Chittee Yoholo; Creek chief McIntosh; Cherokee leader David Vann; and Choctaw chief Pushmataha

Of these five tribes, the Cherokee nation was the group whose lifestyle was most like that of Europeans. Realizing that the whites were here to stay, the Cherokee had chosen cultural accommodation, or peaceful compromise, with white society. They tried to combine the best elements of European and Cherokee culture.

Years earlier, the Cherokee had dominated a huge territory in the Southeast. A long series of wars and treaties with the white settlers shrank that area, and by the early 1800s, the Cherokee were confined to northern Georgia.

Their land was fertile, however, and the

A map showing where the Cherokee and other Indian tribes have lived at various times; the triangle-shaped area in the southeast was the land held by the Cherokee before they were forced to move to Oklahoma.

THE CHEROKEE
AND THEIR NEIGHBORS

SHOWING THE TERRITORY HELD
BY THEM AT VARIOUS TIMES
WEST OF THE MISSISSIPPI RIVER
BY
JAMES MOONEY
1900

Note–The territory of the cognate
Iroquoian tribes is indicated
by shaded boundaries

Cherokee homes in the early 1800s

Cherokee nation thrived. Many Cherokee owned small but productive farms. A few owned vast cotton plantations. Still more gathered together and built small towns complete with stores, churches, and schools. One white missionary, writing in 1808, claimed: "Thus far are the Cherokees advanced; farther I believe than any other nation or tribe in America."

The Cherokee so emulated the whites of the Old South that they even adopted the practice of keeping black slaves. A few Cherokee-owned plantations employed as many as a hundred slaves. Medium-sized farms had between twenty and fifty slaves. Many Cherokee households kept just one or two slaves.

Over the years, many Cherokee married white settlers. Scottish and Irish family names such as Taylor, MacGregor, Lowrey, Smith, McCoy, and Montgomery were common within the tribe.

The Cherokee's desire to educate their youth was almost as powerful as a religious belief. Tribal leaders were haunted by memories of Indians who had been cheated of their lands because they could not read the treaties they signed. One Cherokee elder, addressing a grade-school class, warned, "Remember, the whites are near us. . . . Unless you can speak their language

Sequoya invented a Cherokee alphabet to enable his people to read and write in their own language.

Cherokee Alphabet.

Before long, Sequoya's alphabet (left) was being used to produce the Cherokee Phoenix (right), *an English/Cherokee newspaper.*

and read and write as they do, they will be able to cheat you and trample on your rights. Be diligent therefore in your studies."

Reading and writing in the Cherokee language was made possible by a remarkable alphabet invented by a Cherokee named Sequoya. The spoken Cherokee language is a complex combination of sounds strange to the untrained ear. Working painstakingly with a worn pen, Sequoya tried to put the Cherokee tongue into readable symbols. "It was like catching a wild animal and taming it," he once said. In 1821, after twelve years of effort, Sequoya perfected an alphabet of eighty-six characters. The system was amazingly easy to learn, even for old people who

The Cherokee Phoenix *was printed in this building in New Echota, Georgia. New Echota was the Cherokee capital from 1825 to 1838.*

had never been to school. The written language was so popular that before long, the *Cherokee Phoenix,* a newspaper printed in both English and Cherokee, circulated everywhere.

The Cherokee government was modeled after the federal government of the United States. It operated under written laws, and the people elected representatives. When dealing with Washington, the government emphasized friendliness and cooperation. The Cherokee refused to join the anti-Washington alliance proposed by Shawnee leader Tecumseh. The Cherokee even chose to fight alongside white soldiers against their Creek Indian neighbors.

During the Creek War of 1812-13, many Cherokee met an ambitious American general named Andrew Jackson. He would later play a crucial role in the fate of the Cherokee people.

Certainly, the Cherokee nation disproved the charge that Indians were savages unworthy of land ownership. White settlers often used the argument as an excuse to seize Indian territory. Still, the Cherokee fell victim to one of the most shameful episodes of injustice ever committed by the government of the United States. The Cherokee were stripped of the land they so cherished and forced to take a tragic journey that later became known as the Trail of Tears.

Andrew Jackson

The Cherokee Supreme Court building at New Echota

President-elect Andrew Jackson on his way to Washington, D.C.

In 1828, two events shaped the destiny of the Cherokee nation. First, Andrew Jackson was elected president of the United States. Jackson was known as a champion of the common man. But he was first and last a backwoodsman who boasted that he had been born in a log cabin. Like many pioneers, Jackson carried with him a deeply ingrained hostility toward Indians. He could be kind to individual Indians, but as a group, he considered them inferior to and less civilized than whites. Second, gold was discovered at Dahlonega, Georgia, which was in the heart of Cherokee territory. This development had an immediate and dramatic effect on the Cherokee people.

Gold fever swept the South. Miners, hungry for a quick fortune, invaded the Cherokee nation. Many of the miners stole Indian cattle and attacked Indian women. Neighboring whites, who coveted Cherokee land, encouraged the miners. Hoping to harass the Indians into giving up their territory, the whites organized groups called Pony Clubs. These were gangs of rowdies who rode into Cherokee country to start fires and plunder homes.

Many young Cherokee wanted to fight the white invaders. But the older men knew that any act of violence on the part of the Indians would give the state government and President Jackson the excuse they needed to send soldiers marching

When gold fever swept the South in the late 1820s, hundreds of settlers rushed to grab Cherokee land.

The interior of the Cherokee Phoenix *printing office*

onto their land. Writing in the *Cherokee Phoenix,* one leader said, "It has been the desire of our enemies that the Cherokees may be urged to some desperate act. Thus far, this desire has never been realized, and we hope . . . this forbearance will continue."

Vowing not to fight, the Cherokee people took their grievances to court. They argued that the federal government had granted them their land by treaty and therefore they should be protected from the gold miners, from their greedy neighbors, and from the government of the state of Georgia, which also wanted their lands. The Georgia court gave the Cherokee no help at all.

THE CASE

OF

THE CHEROKEE NATION

against

THF STATE OF GEORGIA:

ARGUED AND DETERMINED AT

THE SUPREME COURT OF THE UNITED STATES,

JANUARY TERM 1831.

WITH

AN APPENDIX,

Containing the Opinion of Chancellor Kent on the Case ; the Treaties between the United States and the Cherokee Indians ; the Act of Congress of 1802, entitled ' An Act to regulate intercourse with the Indian tribes, &c.'; and the Laws of Georgia relative to the country occupied by the Cherokee Indians, within the boundary of that State.

BY RICHARD PETERS,
COUNSELLOR AT LAW.

Philadelphia:
JOHN GRIGG, 9 NORTH FOURTH STREET.
1831.

Georgia governor George Gilmer (above) refused to acknowledge the rights of the Cherokee people. Still, the Cherokee tried to use legal channels to hold onto their land; eventually, their case made it all the way to the U.S. Supreme Court (left).

Governor George Gilmer summed up his feelings about land treaties with Indians in this statement: "Treaties were expedients by which ignorant, intractable, and savage people were induced without bloodshed to yield up what civilized peoples had a right to possess."

Eventually, a Cherokee lawsuit reached the United States Supreme Court, the highest court in the land. After a series of decisions, the court ruled in 1832 that the federal government must protect the Cherokee nation from its many intruders. But only the president of the United States had the authority to send troops to ward

Even though the Supreme Court, led by Chief Justice John Marshall (right), upheld the Cherokees' right to keep their land, President Jackson still went ahead with his plan of Indian Removal.

off the invaders of Cherokee land. At the time, President Jackson was preparing for his second term. He refused to help Indians in a conflict against whites. Also, Supreme Court justice John Marshall was his political enemy. In a historic defiance of the Supreme Court's authority, President Jackson proclaimed, "John Marshall has rendered his decision; now let him enforce it."

Moreover, President Jackson considered even harsher methods of dealing with Indians. For almost three decades, government leaders had discussed a plan called Indian Removal. It called for the removal, by force if necessary, of all

Indians east of the Mississippi River. The Indians were to be resettled on land west of the river. Actually, this form of migration had been going on for generations. Many northern tribes had already quietly retreated westward in order to avoid further conflicts with the whites. But in the South, the Five Civilized Tribes clung tenaciously to their territories while white frontiersmen demanded their removal.

Raising the question of Indian Removal, President Jackson told Congress: "I suggest for your consideration the propriety of setting apart an ample district west of the Mississippi . . . to be guaranteed to the Indian tribes as long as they

Indians migrating westward in the early 1800s

Cherokee leaders John Ross (right) and Major Ridge (far right)

shall occupy it." Jackson's pioneer supporters cheered his every word. Under his leadership, the Indian Removal Act became the law of the land.

A feeling of gloom hung like a stubborn fog over the Cherokee nation. Many people simply could not believe that the Indian Removal Act had actually been passed by Congress. The Cherokee land had been guaranteed to the tribe by a treaty endorsed by the federal government. Cherokee people had lived there for countless generations before the coming of the whites. Also, the Cherokee were a community of farmers, not nomadic hunters who could pack up and move at the government's decree.

A debate raged among tribal leaders. One leader, John Ross, wanted to fight removal through the courts. Another, the elderly Major Ridge, urged the people to move to the West

18

Miners rushed to the scene after gold was discovered at Dahlonega, Georgia, in the heart of Cherokee territory.

because he felt that President Jackson's position was unshakable. Hundreds of Cherokee families made plans to hide in caves in the remote hills. Others simply gave up and trekked to the West before they were ordered to do so.

Meanwhile, Georgia authorities and the land-hungry white frontiersmen lay like vultures outside the Cherokee boundaries. Even while the many cases were being argued in court, the state

Mosholotubee, chief of the Choctaw at the time of their removal from the southeast

of Georgia organized a lottery to distribute Cherokee land. Lucky winners were given 160-acre farms or 40-acre mining sites, all to be parceled out just as soon as the Indians were forced off their territory. A popular song of the time began with the words:

> All I want in this creation
> Is a pretty little wife and a big plantation
> Way down yonder in the Cherokee Nation.

In other parts of the South, the Indian Removal Act crushed the Five Civilized Tribes. During the bitter winter of 1831, the migration of the Choctaw began. Many were barefoot, and most had no coats or blankets. Yet they were forced to cross the Mississippi River in zero-degree weather. The federal government had agreed to feed and clothe the Indians during

A painting portraying the Choctaw removal

Of the so-called Five Civilized Tribes, only the Seminole used warfare to resist the American government's order to move westward.

their journey, but money for the provisions was never sent. The Creek were driven out of their homes in 1836. Those who resisted were put in chains and marched double file by United States soldiers. Some thirty-five hundred Creek who started the trek died of hunger and exposure before they reached their new territory. In 1837, the Chickasaw loaded their belongings into wagons and began their sad journey westward. Only the Seminole chose to fight. However, after a long and bloody war, most members of that tribe were herded to the West as well.

By battling through the courts, the Cherokee people resisted migration until 1838. That year, however, the federal government acted on a treaty agreement that had been made two years earlier. Its terms gave away all Cherokee lands east of the Mississippi in exchange for new lands in the West and a cash settlement. But the agreement had been signed by only a tiny minority of the Cherokee people. Some of the signers had been bribed by government officials. Still, the federal government insisted that the treaty was valid.

The month of May 1838 was the beginning of a long nightmare for the Cherokee people. General Winfield Scott, who would later run for president, led an army of seven hundred troops into Cherokee territory—nearly one soldier for every two Cherokee. Without warning, the troops burst into Cherokee homes, dragged the people outside, and drove them toward staging camps. Anyone moving too slowly was prodded by a soldier's bayonet.

Following almost on the heels of the soldiers came neighboring whites who swept up the Cherokee's personal possessions just as soon as the soldiers had forced the Indians from their homes. Like pirates, the whites stuffed sacks with pots, pans, silverware, and musical instruments,

General Winfield Scott was the American officer who supervised the Cherokee removal.

all looted from Cherokee houses and cabins. Fistfights, knife fights, and pistol duels broke out over the booty. Some of the whites, knowing that the Indians often buried their dead with gold and silver jewelry, dug up graves and sifted through decaying corpses searching for treasure.

On June 16, 1838, a Baptist minister named Evan Jones reported, "The Cherokees are nearly all prisoners. They had been dragged from their houses and encamped at the forts and military places, all over the nation. Multitudes were allowed no time to take anything with them except the clothes they had on. Females . . . are driven on foot before the bayonets of brutal men. . . . It is the work of war in time of peace."

Dismayed and in disbelief, the Cherokee wandered about the camps as if in a daze. Many of the white troops who guarded the Indians felt shamed by their duties. "I [later] fought through the War between the States," wrote one infantryman, "and I saw men shot to pieces by the thousands, but the Cherokee Removal was the cruelest work I ever knew."

The staging camps held an estimated seventeen thousand Cherokee. They included sick people, disabled people, elderly men and women, crying babies, and children. Some were put on riverboats for the trip west. Others were led away from the camps in small parties. But the majority of Cherokee made the long, bitter walk to the West together, along a path they called *Nunna-da-ul-tsun-yi*. In the Cherokee language this means, "The place where they cried." History would remember the trek as the Trail of Tears.

On a June morning, a long, ragged column of Cherokee began their westward march. Some of the Indians rode horses or wagons, but the majority walked. A Cherokee named William Coodey later wrote, "Groups of persons formed about each wagon. The day was bright and beautiful, but a gloomy thoughtfulness was depicted in the lineaments of every face. . . . [Suddenly] a low sound of distant thunder fell on

The Trail of Tears, *by Robert Lindneux*

my ears. . . . A dark spiral cloud was rising above the horizon and sent forth a murmur [like] a voice of divine indignation for the wrong of my poor and unhappy countrymen, driven by brutal power from all they loved and cherished in the land of their fathers."

Behind the Cherokee spread the red Georgia clay and the land they had known for generations. Ahead lay an area in present-day Oklahoma that the people had never seen before. The government called the area Indian Territory.

A map showing the route of the Trail of Tears

In between stretched more than eight hundred miles of forests, mountains, swamps, and tortuous wilderness roads.

Every day, the sun raged like a branding iron in the heavens. The countryside suffered from drought. The Cherokee prayed for rain, but none came. Streams and creeks dried to sand, and the people's throats burned with thirst. Still they marched. And every step took them farther away from their homeland.

Diseases such as measles and whooping cough spread from one marcher to another. Frontier settlers who saw the once-proud Cherokee nation pass sadly in front of their homes wrote their relatives back East, "The poor people. They are dying like flies."

Winter struck. It was as cold and forbidding as the summer had been broiling. A howling wind engulfed the people in snow and sleet. A traveler from the state of Maine passed a Cherokee camp and wrote home, "Aging females, apparently nearly ready to drop into the grave, were traveling with heavy burdens attached to their backs—on the frozen ground with no covering for their feet except what nature had given them. We learned from the inhabitants on the road where the Indians passed that they buried fourteen or fifteen at each stopping place."

When winter came, the Cherokee were expected to keep on marching.

The 800-mile journey was so harsh and difficult that a quarter of the marchers died along the route.

*After they were relocated to Indian Territory, the Cherokee set up
their capital at Tahlequah, Oklahoma. This school for Cherokee girls
was established in Tahlequah in 1888.*

It took more than a year for all the people to
travel the full length of the Trail of Tears and
reach Oklahoma. It is estimated that one of every
four of the Cherokee who started the 800-mile
march from Georgia died along the route.

The heartbreak of the Cherokee did not end
with the Trail of Tears. The federal government
had granted the land in Oklahoma to the
Cherokee and the other Indian tribes for "as long
as the grass shall grow and the streams shall
run." But just a few years after the Indians were
resettled, white pioneers began to probe into
their territory. The federal government did little
to discourage them. After the Civil War, the white

Opposite page: A waterfall in the part of Georgia that was once Cherokee territory

invaders became a horde. Parcel by parcel, the federal government bought up or seized Indian territory and opened it officially to white farmers. By the turn of the century, the Indian nations in Oklahoma held almost no land at all.

In Georgia, the Cherokee people had not been completely eradicated. A few hundred Cherokee had avoided General Scott's roundup by hiding in the hills. One of them, a man named Tsali, became a legend. Even today, the Cherokee tell his story.

Tsali killed a white soldier after he saw the soldier jabbing a bayonet at Tsali's wife. General Scott, the officer in charge, knew it would be difficult to capture Tsali and to flush out the hundreds of other Cherokee who resisted migration by living in caves. So Scott sent word to Tsali that if he would give himself up, the army would abandon its efforts to find other Indians hiding in the hills. Tsali agreed to the terms and surrendered to Scott. He was sentenced to death for killing the soldier.

On a warm summer morning, Tsali faced a firing squad. As a final act of cruelty, the army forced Cherokee prisoners to serve as his executioners. Tsali refused a blindfold. Instead, he spent his final instant on this earth gazing at the red clay of the old Cherokee nation. It is said that his last words were, "It is sweet to die in one's own country."

INDEX

PHOTO CREDITS

Cover, Barthell Little Chief; 1, Lake Region Electric Cooperative-Hulbert; 2, © J. H. Robinson/Root Resources; 3, 4, North Wind; 5, The Thomas Gilcrease Institute of American History and Art, Tulsa, Oklahoma; 6, North Carolina State Archives; 7, Archives & Manuscripts Division of the Oklahoma Historical Society; 8, Historical Pictures/Stock Montage; 9 (left), North Wind; 9 (right), Archives & Manuscripts Division of the Oklahoma Historical Society; 10, 11 (bottom), Georgia Department of Industry and Trade; 11 (top), Bureau of Engraving and Printing; 12, North Wind; 13, Western History Collections, University of Oklahoma Library; 14, Georgia Department of Industry and Trade; 15, North Wind; 16, Historical Pictures/Stock Montage; 17, North Wind; 18 (left), Historical Pictures/Stock Montage; 18 (right), The Thomas Gilcrease Institute of American History and Art, Tulsa, Oklahoma; 19, North Wind; 20 (top), The Bettmann Archive; 20 (bottom), The Philbrook Museum of Art, Tulsa, Oklahoma; 21, North Wind; 23, Historical Pictures/Stock Montage; 25, Woolaroc Museum, Bartlesville, Oklahoma; 26, North Carolina State Archives; 27, Rick Regan; 28, La Gere & Walkingstick Insurance Agency; 29, Archives & Manuscripts Division of the Oklahoma Historical Society; 31, © Richard Jacobs/Root Resources

Picture Identifications:
Cover: A depiction of the Trail of Tears by Barthell Little Chief
Page 1: *Trail of Tears,* by Solomon McCombs
Page 2: A view from Black Rock Mountain in northern Georgia

Project Editor: Shari Joffe
Designer: Karen Yops
Photo Editor: Jan Izzo
Cornerstones of Freedom Logo: David Cunningham

ABOUT THE AUTHOR

R. Conrad Stein was born and raised in Chicago. He enlisted in the Marine Corps at the age of eighteen and served for three years. He then attended the University of Illinois, where he received a bachelor's degree in history. He later studied in Mexico, earning an advanced degree from the University of Guanajuato. Mr. Stein is the author of many books, articles, and short stories for young people.

Mr. Stein lives in Chicago with his wife and their daughter Janna.